Lesson Plans

K-2, 3-5, 6-8

by Dr. Darling J. Miramey

Kościuszko Day, celebrated annually on October 15th, honors Tadeusz Kościuszko, a Polish and American hero known for his contributions to the fight for freedom and independence. In schools, we celebrate this day to instill in students the values of patriotism, courage, and the pursuit of liberty. This lesson will support our celebration by exploring Kościuszko's life and achievements, highlighting his impact on both Polish and American history. Through engaging activities and discussions, students will gain a deeper understanding of the significance of Kościuszko's legacy and the importance of standing up for freedom and justice.

Notes:

Lesson Plan 1:

Lower Elementary (Grades K-2) 35-40 min.

Title: Kościuszko's Adventure: A Helping Hero

SWBAT:

- Identify Tadeusz Kościuszko as a historical figure who helped others by participating in an interactive storytelling activity.

- Describe at least one way Kościuszko helped others by sharing their understanding with the class.

- Create a "Helping Hero" badge and explain how they can help others in their own lives by presenting their badge to the class.

NATIONAL/NY STATE CORE STANDARDS:

- CCSS.ELA-Literacy.SL.K-2.1: Participate in collaborative conversations with diverse partners about grade-level topics and texts with peers and adults in small and larger groups.

- CCSS.ELA-Literacy.SL.K-2.4: Describe people, places, things, and events with relevant details, expressing ideas and feelings clearly.

MATERIALS:

Props for storytelling (e.g., hats, toy swords, maps, sticks, stones, ropes)
"Helping Hero" prepare badges Art supplies

Notes:

Book Resources and Story Options

Book or narrative story about helping others (e.g., "A Sick Day for Amos McGee," "The Giving Tree," "Should I Share My Ice Cream?" or "Kosciuszko's Helping Heart")

"A Sick Day for Amos McGee" by Philip C. Stead

Summary: This story follows Amos McGee, a friendly zookeeper who always makes time for his animal friends. When Amos is too sick to go to work, his friends come to visit him and take care of him.

Connection to Lesson: This book emphasizes the importance of helping others and the value of friendship, which can be related to how Kościuszko helped others throughout his life.

"The Giving Tree" by Shel Silverstein

Summary: This classic tale follows the life of a boy and a tree, with the tree always giving to the boy throughout his life.

Connection to Lesson: The story highlights selflessness and the act of giving, which can be connected to Kościuszko's contributions and his dedication to helping others.

"Should I Share My Ice Cream?" by Mo Willems

Summary: In this story, Gerald the elephant faces a dilemma when he has to decide whether to share his ice cream with his friend Piggie.

Connection to Lesson: This book teaches about sharing and the importance of helping friends, which can be related to Kościuszko's actions and the concept of being a "Helping Hero."

Notes:

Kościuszko's Story
Title: "Kościuszko's Helping Heart"

Once upon a time, in a faraway land, there lived a brave and kind man named Tadeusz Kościuszko. Kościuszko was known for his big heart and his desire to help others. He traveled from place to place, always looking for ways to make people's lives better.

One day, Kościuszko arrived in a small village where the people were very sad. Their bridge had been washed away by a storm, and they couldn't cross the river to get to the market or visit their friends. Kościuszko saw their sadness and decided to help. He gathered the villagers and asked them to bring all the materials they could find— sticks, stones, and ropes.

Together, they worked hard to build a new bridge. Kościuszko used his engineering skills to make sure the bridge was strong and safe. When the bridge was finally finished, the villagers cheered with joy. They could now cross the river and go about their daily lives. Kościuszko's kindness and hard work had brought happiness back to the village.

From that day forward, Kościuszko continued to travel and help others. He built bridges, fortified towns, and even fought in battles to protect people's freedom. His helping heart made him a hero to many, and his legacy of kindness and bravery lived on.

Connection to Lesson: This story emphasizes the importance of helping others and using one's skills to make a positive impact, which aligns with the theme of Tadeusz Kościuszko's life and contributions.

Notes:

Lesson Procedure

Introduction (5 minutes)

• Introduce Tadeusz Kościuszko as a hero who helped others.
• Show students his portrait and briefly discuss his story.

Storytelling (10 minutes)

Preparation (2 minutes):

• Gather the props needed for the story (e.g., hats for characters, toy swords for soldiers, maps for travel, sticks, stones, and ropes for building).
• Assign roles to students or have them volunteer for different parts (e.g., Kosciuszko, villagers, soldiers, animals).

Interactive Reading (8 minutes):

• Begin reading the chosen book or the narrative story "Kościuszko's Helping Heart" to the class.
• Pause at key moments in the story to encourage students to act out the scenes using the props. For example: When Kościuszko arrives in the village, have a student wear a hat and mimic his actions. When the villagers are sad, have students make sad faces and act out their distress. When Kościuszko and the villagers build the bridge, have students use sticks, stones, and ropes to mimic the building process. Encourage students to use their imagination and be creative with the props. Ask questions to engage students, such as "What do you think Kościuszko should do next?" or "How can the villagers help Kościuszko build the bridge?"

Notes:

Discussion and Activities

Discussion (5 minutes)

- After the story, discuss how Kościuszko helped others and how students can be helping heroes in their own lives.

- Ask questions like, "How did Kościuszko help the villagers?" and "What can we do to help others like Kosciuszko did?"

Badge Creation (10 minutes)

- Students create their own "Helping Hero" badges using art supplies.

- Encourage students to design their badges to reflect how they can help others.

Wrap-up (5 minutes)

- Sharing (3 minutes): Students share how they can help others, like Kościuszko did, by presenting their badges to the class.

- Display (2 minutes): Display the badges in the classroom as a reminder of their commitment to helping others. With eventual documentation by making photos and sharing with community.

- Clean-up.

Notes:

Optional Song Activities

"Kindness Song" by Jack Hartmann

Lyrics Sample: "Kindness is sharing, kindness is caring, kindness is being a friend..."

Connection: This song emphasizes the importance of kindness and helping others, which aligns with the theme of Tadeusz Kosciuszko's life.

"The Helping Song" by The Kiboomers

Lyrics Sample: "Helping each other, that's what friends do, helping each other, we can make it through..."

Connection: This song highlights the value of helping others and the importance of friendship, which can be related to Kościuszko's actions.

"What a Wonderful World" by Louis Armstrong (Kids Version)

Lyrics Sample: "I see trees of green, red roses too, I see them bloom, for me and you..."

Connection: While not directly about helping others, this song encourages appreciation for the world and the people in it, which can inspire kindness and helpfulness.

"The Friendship Song" by The Laurie Berkner Band

Lyrics Sample: "We're friends, we're friends, we're friends together, we're friends, we're friends, we're friends forever..."

Connection: This song emphasizes the importan-ce of friendship and being there for each other, which can be related to the theme of helping others.

"The More We Get Together" (Traditional)

Lyrics Sample: "The more we get together, together, together, the more we get together, the happier we'll be..."

Connection: This traditional song encourages unity and togetherness, which can be connected to the idea of helping and supporting each other.

Notes:

Song Integration Options

How to Incorporate the Songs into the Lesson (options):

1	2	3

Introduction

Play one of the songs at the beginning of the lesson to set a positive and engaging tone. Discuss the lyrics and how they relate to the theme of helping others.

During the Activity

Play the song softly in the background while students are creating their "Helping Hero" badges to maintain a positive and creative atmosphere.

Wrap-up

Play the song again at the end of the lesson and encourage students to sing along. Discuss how the song's message relates to what they learned about Tadeusz Kościuszko and the importance of helping others.

Notes:

Badge Making Supplies

Art Supplies for "Helping Hero" Badges:

Pre-cut Circles

Purpose: Serve as the base for the badges.

Preparation: Cut out circles from construction paper or cardstock ahead of time. Choose a size that is appropriate for a badge (e.g., 3-4 inches in diameter).

Stickers

Purpose: For adding decorative elements to the badges.

Preparation: Provide sheets of colorful stickers in various sizes.

Markers or Crayons

Purpose: For drawing and coloring designs on the badges.

Preparation: Ensure you have a variety of colors available.

Googly Eyes

Purpose: To add a fun and creative touch to the badges.

Preparation: Provide googly eyes in different sizes.

Notes:

Badge Making Supplies (Part 2)

Additional Art Supplies for "Helping Hero" Badges:

Pom-poms

Purpose: For adding texture and decoration to the badges.

Preparation: Have a variety of colors and sizes available.

Yarn or String

Purpose: To create a loop for wearing the badge.

Preparation: Cut yarn or string into lengths suitable for making loops ahead of time.

Glue

Purpose: For attaching decorative elements to the badges.

Preparation: Have glue sticks or liquid glue available for students.

Safety Pins (Optional)

Purpose: Alternative method for attaching badges to clothing.

Preparation: Have safety pins available if you prefer this method over yarn loops.

Notes:

Badge Creation Instructions
Instructions for Creating the Badges:

01

Prepare the Base

Provide each student with a pre-cut circle to serve as the base for their badge.

02

Design the Badge

Encourage students to think about how they can help others, like Tadeusz Kościuszko did. Have students draw and color designs on their badges using markers or crayons. They can include symbols or words that represent helping and kindness.

03

Add Decorative Elements

Students can use stickers, googly eyes, and pom-poms to add decorative elements to their badges. Remind students to use glue to attach these elements securely.

04

Create a Loop

Help students create a loop using pre-cut yarn or string so they can wear their badges. Attach the loop to the back of the badge using tape.

05

Share and Display

Once the badges are complete, have students share how they can help others by presenting their badges to the class. Display the badges in the classroom as a reminder of their commitment to helping others.

Notes:

Teaching Tips for K-2 Activities

Tips for Teachers:

- Pre-cut Materials: To save time, pre-cut the bases for the badges and any other materials that require cutting.

- Demonstrate: Show students examples of completed badges or create a sample badge to inspire their designs.

- Encourage Creativity: Encourage students to be creative and express their unique ideas on their badges.

- Positive Reinforcement: Praise students for their efforts and creativity to boost their confidence and engagement.

Tips for Encouraging Student Participation:

- Model the Actions: Before asking students to act out parts of the story, demonstrate the actions yourself to give them a clear idea of what to do.

- Positive Reinforcement: Praise students for their participation and creativity. This will encourage more students to volunteer and engage in the activity.

- Inclusive Environment: Ensure that all students feel comfortable participating. You can do this by creating a supportive and inclusive classroom environment where everyone's contributions are valued.

- Adapt for Different Abilities: Be mindful of students with different abilities and adapt the activity as needed. For example, students who are less comfortable acting out scenes can participate by holding props or narrating parts of the story.

Notes:

Lesson Plan 2:

Upper Elementary (Grades 3-5) 45 min
Title: Engineering Peace: Kosciuszko's Forts and Bridges
– The Marshmallow Challenge

SWBAT:

- Describe Tadeusz Kościuszko's engineering contributions to both Poland and the United States by creating a poster or presentation.

- Build a fort or bridge using provided materials to solve a specific engineering challenge by working collaboratively in groups.

- Test the strength and stability of their constructions by participating in a "Marshmallow Test of Construction" using rulers and marshmallows as "projectiles."

- Explain how their design choices addressed the engineering challenge by presenting their structure to the class.

- Relate the activity to modern engineering challenges and the role of engineers in keeping people safe by participating in a class discussion.

Notes:

Standards and Materials for Upper Elementary Lesson

This section outlines the core standards addressed by the lesson plan and the materials required for the "Engineering Peace: Kościuszko's Forts and Bridges – The Marshmallow Challenge" activity.

NATIONAL/NY STATE CORE STANDARDS:

- CCSS.ELA-Literacy.W.3-5.7: Conduct short research projects that build knowledge about a topic.

- CCSS.ELA-Literacy.SL.3-5.4: Report on a topic or text, tell a story, or recount an experience in an organized manner, using appropriate facts and relevant, descriptive details to support main ideas or themes; speak clearly at an understandable pace.

- NGSS.3-5-ETS1-1: Define a simple design problem reflecting a need or a want that includes specified criteria for success and constraints on materials, time, or cost.

- NGSS.3-5-ETS1-2: Generate and compare multiple possible solutions to a problem based on how well each is likely to meet the criteria and constraints of the problem.

MATERIALS:

- Books and articles about Kosciuszko

- Building materials (e.g., LEGO, K'NEX, or recycled materials)

- "Engineering Challenge" cards

- Rulers

- Marshmallows (as "projectiles")

- Poster board and markers (optional)

Notes:

Lesson Procedure (Part 1)

Introduction (10minutes)

Reading (5minutes): Read about Tadeusz Kościuszko and his engineering contributions. Students will take notes on Kościuszko's engineering achievements.

Discussion (5 minutes): Discuss how engineers help solve problems and keep people safe. Students will share their notes with the class.

Activity (17 minutes)

Group Formation (3 minutes): Divide students into groups.

Challenge Assignment (2 minutes): Each group draws an "Engineering Challenge" card with a specific problem to solve (e.g., build a bridge that can hold the most weight, or design a fort that can withstand a "marshmallow projectile" test). Students will read the challenge and discuss their plan with their group.

Building (12 minutes): Students work in groups to build a fort or bridge using the provided materials. Students will collaborate to design and build their structure, considering strength and stability.

Notes:

Lesson Procedure (Part 2)

Testing and Discussion (8 minutes)

Marshmallow Test of Construction (5 minutes): Groups take turns trying to test each other's constructions using rulers and marshmallows as "projectiles." Students will aim marshmallows at the structures using rulers as catapults.

Discussion (3 minutes): After the test, groups discuss their design choices and how well their structures held up. Students will explain how their design addressed the engineering challenge and what they would do differently next time.

Wrap-up (10 minutes)

Presentation (7 minutes): Each group presents their structure and explains their design choices. Students will present their structure to the class and explain how their design addressed the engineering challenge and how it performed during the Marshmallow Test of Construction.

Class Discussion (3 minutes): Relate the activity to modern engineering challenges and the role of engineers in keeping people safe.

Notes:

Engineering Challenge Cards (Part 1)

Bridge Builder

Challenge: Build a bridge that can hold the most weight using the provided materials.

- The bridge must span a gap of at least 10 inches.
- The bridge must support a weight of at least 500 grams without collapsing.
- The bridge should be stable and not wobble when weight is applied.

Fort Defender

Challenge: Design a fort that can withstand a "marshmallow projectile" test.

- The fort must have walls that are at least 6 inches high.
- The fort must withstand at least 5 direct hits from marshmallows launched with a ruler.
- The fort should remain standing and not collapse under the projectile test.

Tower of Strength

Challenge: Construct a tower that is as tall as possible while remaining stable.

- The tower must be at least 12 inches tall.
- The tower must remain standing for at least 1 minute without any external support.
- The tower should not sway or lean significantly when lightly touched.

Balancing Act

Challenge: Build a balanced structure that can support a weight on a single point.

- The structure must have a single point of contact with the ground.
- The structure must support a weight of at least 100 grams without tipping over.
- The structure should remain balanced for at least 30 seconds.

Notes:

Engineering Challenge Cards (Part 2)

Suspension Bridge

Challenge:

Design a suspension bridge that can hold a weight without sagging.

- The bridge must span a gap of at least 12 inches.

- The bridge must support a weight of at least 300 grams without the middle sagging more than 1 inch.

- The bridge should be stable and not sway excessively when weight is applied.

Protective Shield

Challenge:

Create a shield that can protect an object from falling marshmallows.

- The shield must cover an area of at least 6 inches by 6 inches.

- The shield must protect the object from at least 10 falling marshmallows.

- The shield should remain intact and not break under the impact of the marshmallows.

Notes:

Engineering Challenge Cards (Part 3)

Arch Builder

Challenge:

Construct an arch that can support a weight without collapsing.

- The arch must span a gap of at least 8 inches.

- The arch must support a weight of at least 200 grams without collapsing.

- The arch should be stable and not wobble when weight is applied.

Cantilever Challenge

Challenge:

Build a cantilever structure that can extend as far as possible without collapsing.

- The cantilever must extend at least 8 inches from the base.

- The cantilever must support a weight of at least 100 grams at the end without collapsing.

- The structure should be stable and not wobble when weight is applied.

Notes:

Assessment and Extensions
Additional Tips:

Differentiation:

Scaffolding: Provide additional support for students who may struggle with the building or presentation aspects. Offer templates or examples to guide them.

Challenge: For advanced students, offer additional challenges or constraints to push their critical thinking skills.

Assessment:

Observation: Observe students during the activity to assess their collaboration, problem-solving, and critical thinking skills.

Rubric: Use a rubric to evaluate the presentations, focusing on clarity, organization, and the application of engineering principles.

Extension Activities:

Poster Presentation: Encourage students to create posters about Kościuszko's engineering contributions as an extension activity.

Research Project: Assign a short research project where students can explore other historical figures who made significant engineering contributions.

Notes:

Teaching Tips and Guidelines (Part 1)

Preparation:

1. **Gather Materials:** Ensure you have all the necessary materials, including books, articles, building materials, rulers, marshmallows, and poster board with markers.

2. **Prepare "Engineering Challenge" Cards:** Create cards with specific engineering challenges such as "build a bridge that can hold the most weight" or "design a fort that can withstand a marshmallow projectile test."

3. **Review Content:** Familiarize yourself with Tadeusz Kościuszko's engineering contributions to effectively guide the discussion and answer student questions.

Introduction (10 minutes):

1. **Engage Students:** Start with an engaging hook, such as a brief story about Kościuszko or a visual of one of his engineering feats.

2. **Note-Taking:** Encourage students to take notes on key points about Kościuszko's achievements. Provide a note-taking template if needed.

3. **Facilitate Discussion:** Ask open-ended questions to encourage students to share their thoughts on how engineers solve problems and keep people safe.

Notes:

Teaching Tips and Guidelines (Part 2)
Activity (25 minutes):

1

Group Formation

Divide students into groups of 3-4 to ensure balanced participation. Consider mixing abilities to foster collaboration.

2

Challenge Assignment

Clearly explain the rules and objectives of the challenge. Ensure each group understands their specific task before they start building.

3

Building

Time Management: Use a timer to keep students on track. Remind them of the time remaining periodically.

Collaboration: Encourage students to discuss their plans and divide tasks within their groups.

Problem-Solving: Circulate among the groups to offer guidance and ask probing questions to help students think critically about their designs.

4

Testing and Discussion

Marshmallow Test: Ensure safety by setting clear rules for the marshmallow test. Emphasize that the goal is to test the structures, not to compete aggressively.

Reflection: After the test, guide students in reflecting on their design choices. Ask questions like, "What worked well?" and "What would you change next time?"

Notes:

Wrap-up (10 minutes)

1. Presentation:

- **Structure:** Provide a clear structure for the presentations, such as introducing the challenge, explaining the design choices, and discussing the test results.

- **Time Management:** Use a timer to ensure each group has an equal amount of time to present.

2. Class Discussion:

- **Modern Engineering:** Relate the activity to modern engineering challenges. Use examples of current engineering projects that aim to keep people safe.

- **Student Engagement:** Encourage students to share their thoughts on the role of engineers in society and how they can contribute to solving real-world problems.

Notes:

Additional Teaching Tips
for Grades 3-5

Differentiation

Scaffolding: Provide additional support for students who may struggle with the building or presentation aspects. Offer templates or examples to guide them.

Challenge: For advanced students, offer additional challenges or constraints to push their critical thinking skills.

Assessment

Observation: Observe students during the activity to assess their collaboration, problem-solving, and critical thinking skills.

Rubric: Use a rubric to evaluate the presentations, focusing on clarity, organization, and the application of engineering principles.

Extension Activities

Poster Presentation: Encourage students to create posters about Kościuszko's engineering contributions as an extension activity.

Research Project: Assign a short research project where students can explore other historical figures who made significant engineering contributions.

Notes:

Lesson Plan 3:

Middle School (Grades 6-8)

Title: "Kościuszko: Freedom Fighter and Modern Strategies"

SWBAT:

- Analyze the life and contributions of Tadeusz Kościuszko and understand his impact on the fight for freedom and democracy by conducting research and creating a presentation or infographic.

- Research and analyze the strategies used by Kościuszko in his fight for freedom by working collaboratively in groups.

- Relate Kościuszko's strategies to modern conflicts and discuss their relevance by participating in a class discussion.

- Create a presentation or infographic to share their findings by presenting their work to the class.

NATIONAL/NY STATE CORE STANDARDS:

- CCSS.ELA-Literacy.W.6-8.7: Conduct short research projects to answer a question (including a self-generated question), drawing on several sources and generating additional related, focused questions that allow for multiple avenues of exploration.

- CCSS.ELA-Literacy.SL.6-8.4: Present claims and findings, sequencing ideas logically and using pertinent descriptions, facts, and details to accentuate main ideas or themes; use appropriate eye contact, adequate volume, and clear pronunciation.

- NY.6-8.SS.1: Students will examine the historical development of American culture, its evolution, plurality, and diversity, and compare and contrast American culture to other cultures.

MATERIALS:

- Biographies and articles about Kosciuszko
- Computers or tablets for research
- "Strategy Cards"
- "Current Events" articles

Notes:

Lesson Procedure (Part 1)

Introduction (10 minutes)

Overview (5 minutes): Provide a brief overview of Tadeusz Kościuszko's life and accomplishments. Students will take notes on Kościuszko's life and achievements.

Discussion (5 minutes): Discuss the significance of Kościuszko Day and his role as a freedom fighter. Students will share their notes with the class.

Activity (35 minutes)

Group Formation (3 minutes): Divide students into groups.

Strategy Assignment (2 minutes): Each group receives a "Strategy Card" with a specific strategy to focus on. Students will read the strategy and discuss their plan with their group.

Research (15 minutes): Students research and analyze the strategies used by Kościuszko in his fight for freedom. Students will conduct research using computers or tablets and take notes on their findings.

Notes:

Lesson Procedure (Part 2)

Activity (continued)

Current Events Analysis (10 minutes): Students read "Current Events" articles and discuss how Kościuszko's strategies are still used in modern conflicts. Students will analyze the articles and discuss their findings with their group.

Presentation Preparation (5 minutes): Groups create a presentation or infographic to share their findings. Students will collaborate to create their presentation or infographic.

Wrap-up (15 minutes)

Presentation (10 minutes): Each group presents their findings. Students will present their presentation or infographic to the class and explain their findings.

Class Discussion (5 minutes): Facilitate a class discussion on the evolution of war strategies and the importance of understanding historical figures like Kościuszko in the context of modern conflicts. Students will participate in the class discussion by sharing their thoughts and ideas.

Notes:

Strategy Cards and Teaching Tips

Tips for Teachers:

By using these strategy cards, students will gain a deeper understanding of Tadeusz Kościuszko's contributions and the relevance of his strategies in modern conflicts. This approach encourages critical thinking, research skills, and collaborative learning.

Alliance Building

Description:
Kościuszko formed alliances with other nations and leaders to strengthen his cause.

Task:
Research and analyze how Kościuszko built alliances during his military campaigns. Discuss the importance of alliances in modern conflicts.

Questions to Consider:
What were the key alliances Kościuszko formed? How did these alliances benefit his cause? How do modern nations form alliances, and what are the benefits and challenges?

Guerrilla Warfare

Description:
Kościuszko employed guerrilla tactics to fight against larger and more powerful armies.

Task:
Research and analyze the guerrilla warfare strategies used by Kościuszko. Discuss the effectiveness of guerrilla tactics in modern conflicts.

Questions to Consider:
What specific guerrilla tactics did Kościuszko use? How effective were these tactics against his opponents? How are guerrilla tactics used in modern conflicts, and what are the ethical considerations?

Notes:

Diplomacy

Description: Explore how Tadeusz Kościuszko masterfully employed diplomacy, not just as a tool for peace, but as a strategic maneuver to garner international support and navigate complex political landscapes during his campaigns.

Task: Undertake a detailed investigation into Kościuszko's diplomatic initiatives. Analyze his successes and failures in securing crucial alliances and de-escalating tensions. Then, draw parallels to contemporary international relations, evaluating the enduring significance of diplomatic strategies in resolving global crises.

Questions to Consider: Which specific diplomatic missions or negotiations did Kościuszko undertake, and with what objectives? How effective was his approach in gaining allies or mitigating threats? Compare Kościuszko's diplomatic challenges and tactics to those faced by leaders in current geopolitical conflicts. What lessons can be learned about the complexities and ethical dilemmas of modern diplomacy?

Notes:

Strategy Cards (Part 3)

Engineering and Fortification

Description:

Kościuszko's engineering skills were crucial in building fortifications and defending key locations.

Task:

Research and analyze Kościuszko's engineering contributions, such as the fortifications at West Point. Discuss the importance of engineering in modern military strategies.

Questions to Consider:

What specific engineering projects did Kościuszko work on? How did these projects contribute to his military success? How is engineering used in modern military strategies, and what are the advancements?

Inspiring Leadership

Description:

Kościuszko's leadership inspired his followers and motivated them to fight for their cause.

Task:

Research and analyze Kosciuszko's leadership style and its impact on his followers. Discuss the importance of leadership in modern conflicts.

Questions to Consider:

What qualities made Kościuszko an effective leader? How did his leadership inspire his followers? How is leadership important in modern conflicts, and what qualities make an effective leader?

Notes:

Notes:

Notes:

Notes:

Notes:

Notes:

Notes:

Notes:

Notes:

Notes:

Notes:

Notes:

Notes: